Alien Vacation

story by F. R. Robinson
illustrated by Loreen Leedy

HARCOURT BRACE & COMPANY

Orlando   Atlanta   Austin   Boston   San Francisco   Chicago   Dallas   New York
Toronto   London

Where should we go for vacation?

Let's go to a new planet this time.

Having a great time with our Earth cousins!